READING ABOUT ROCKS

by
Robin Twiddy

BookLife PUBLISHING

©2018
BookLife Publishing
King's Lynn
Norfolk PE30 4LS

All rights reserved.
Printed in Malaysia.

A catalogue record for this book is available from the British Library.

ISBN: 978–1–78637–355–7

Written by:
Robin Twiddy

Edited by:
Kirsty Holmes

Designed by:
Gareth Liddington

Photocredits: All images are courtesy of Shutterstock.com.

Cover – Photobac, Kostikova Natalia, Alexander Korobchenko, Daria Serdtseva, Mihai Daniel, 2 – Piotr Zajda, 3 – VladaKela, Wellford Tiller, 4 – Efimova Anna, Wellford Tiller, 5 – Paul B. Moore, 6 – AvDe, 7 – Vitaliy Balenko, vvoe, Breck P. Kent, Schad, Titus and Co, 8 – Vastram, 10 – Walter Bilotta, vvoe, www.sandatlas.org, 11 – allstars, 12 – Alf Maciagli, 13 – www.sandatlas.org, Fokin Oleg, Aleksandr Pobedimskiy, vvoe, 14 – PTCH, 15 – g.art.for.u, Dhanachote Vongprasert, 16 – corlaffra, 17 – JeremyRichards, 18 – Lucky Team Studio, David Fowler, 19 – Richard A McMillin, 20 – prapann, Anastasios71, 21 – Kletr, 22 – Merlin74, 23 – Adwo.

Images are courtesy of Shutterstock.com. With thanks to Getty Images, Thinkstock Photo and iStockphoto.

All facts, statistics, web addresses and URLs in this book were verified as valid and accurate at time of writing.
No responsibility for any changes to external websites or references can be accepted by either the author or publisher.

CONTENTS

Page 4   Rock 'n' Roll
Page 6   Igneous Rock
Page 8   Sedimentary Rock
Page 10 Metamorphic Rock
Page 12 The Rock Cycle
Page 14 Weathering and Erosion
Page 18 Landslides and Sinkholes
Page 20 Using Rocks
Page 22 Fossils
Page 24 Glossary and Index

Words that look like **this** can be found in the glossary on page 24.

ROCK 'N' ROLL

HAVE YOU EVER REALLY THOUGHT ABOUT ROCKS?

Mountains are huge rocks!

Smooth Pebble

This flint arrowhead is over 2 million years old!

Rocks are everywhere. They are under our feet, in our walls and even in outer space. Rocks are really amazing!

Geologists are people who study how rocks are made and what they can tell us about our planet. Even though there are hundreds of different-looking rocks, there are only three rock families.

- Sedimentary
  (say: sed–ih–ment–ary)
- Igneous
  (say: ig–nee–us)
- metamorphic
  (say: met–a–more–fic)

Each one is formed in a different way.

A Geologist

IGNEOUS ROCK

DID YOU KNOW THAT ROCKS CAN MELT?

Igneous rock is made from molten rock. This is rock that has become so hot that it has turned to liquid! When this molten rock cools down, it becomes solid and forms igneous rock.

Can you see where the molten rock is turning black? This is where it is cooling in the air.

There are two types of igneous rock: extrusive and intrusive.

Extrusive Igneous Rock:
- Forms on the Earth's surface from **lava**
- Cools very quickly
- Forms small crystals

Intrusive Igneous Rock:
- Forms underground from **magma**
- Cools slowly
- Forms large crystals

Andesite

Granite

Diorite

Obsidian

SEDIMENTARY ROCK

HOW ARE SOME ROCKS LIKE CAKES?

The layers are like a cake! They are called strata.

Sedimentary rocks are formed from lots of small pieces of other rocks over a very long period of time. This can take millions of years. These pieces are swept along by the rivers. When they reach a lake or the sea, they are **deposited** at the bottom in layers. This is called sedimentation.

New layers of sediment are deposited on top by the river. The new layer squeezes the bottom layers together. This is called compaction. When this squeezing happens, all the water between the bits of rock is forced out. Salt crystals form, and they act like a glue. This is called cementation.

Material is washed into the sea or blown in by wind.

Sea

Sediment layers form.

Over time, the bottom layers turn into rock.

METAMORPHIC ROCK

HOW DO ROCKS CHANGE?

Metamorphic rocks are made from other types of rock, and have been changed by temperature or **pressure**. This change takes a very long time. Metamorphic rocks are mostly found deep in the Earth, or close to volcanoes.

Marble

All of these metamorphic rocks used to be other kinds of rocks.

Phyllite

Gneiss

Diamonds are formed deep underground where the temperature and pressure are very high.

When rocks are buried deep in the Earth, they come under pressure from the weight of the mud and rocks above them. When this happens, these rocks change. One way that they change is that they grow different types of crystals.

THE ROCK CYCLE

DO ROCKS KEEP CHANGING?

This is a rock core sample showing the different layers of rock.

As we have seen, there are three types of rock: sedimentary, igneous and metamorphic. It may take a million years but one type of rock can become another.

Look at this diagram. It shows how igneous or metamorphic rock can change into sedimentary rock just by being broken down in moving water. Any type of rock can become another type, if there is the right temperature or pressure.

High temperature or pressure creates metamorphic rocks.

SEDIMENTARY

Weathering and erosion (see page 14) creates sedimentary rocks.

METAMORPHIC

IGNEOUS

MAGMA

WEATHERING AND EROSION

CAN A PLANT BE STRONGER THAN A ROCK?

When rocks are worn away, broken down or **dissolved,** it is called weathering. This can happen in different ways. Believe it or not, rocks can be broken down by plants when they grow. This is known as organic weathering.

The roots of a plant can push apart cracks in the rocks.

Freezing water can also damage house bricks.

Water can get inside cracks in rocks. When the water freezes, it gets a little bit bigger. This forces open the crack a little more. Over time, this can cause parts of the rock to come loose. This is known as mechanical weathering.

The acid in the rain has gradually worn away this limestone.

The third type of weathering is chemical. An example of chemical weathering is how water dissolves limestone. Most rainwater is a little bit **acidic**, just like lemon juice. It is not harmful to people but it can make certain rocks wear away. Limestone and chalk both wear away slowly because of the acids in water.

When rocks have been weakened or broken down by weathering, wind or water can move those parts of the rock away. This is called erosion. Erosion can weaken a rock formation and lead to landslides or sink holes (see page 18).

This marble has been eroded by water in Lago General Carrera, Chile.

LANDSLIDES AND SINKHOLES

HOW DOES A LANDSLIDE START?

Erosion on slopes can cause landslides. This is when parts of the rock become loose and begin to fall down the slope. These bits of loose rock can knock other loose rock, and soon lots of weakened and loose rock will fall all together.

Some places have warning signs if the cliffs are very eroded.

A sinkhole is a hole in the ground that is made when **groundwater** weakens the rock. This usually happens if the ground rock is limestone or chalk, which are both easily weathered by rainwater. Some places are more likely to have sinkholes. Florida, in the USA, is on a bed of limestone and has lots of sinkholes.

USING ROCKS

WHAT CAN WE USE ROCKS FOR?

Greek Marble Statue

Stone Age Tool

People have found all sorts of uses for all sorts of rocks. Way back in the past, as far as 2.5 million years ago, early humans started making tools from rocks. Now we have found more and more ways to use rocks for building, art, jewellery and more.

Rocks often contain metals. When they do, they are known as ores. People found that they could take the metal from ores and use this to make better tools. Think about all the metal objects you see and use each day. All of that metal started off as ore buried in rocks.

The **metallic** ore in the rock makes interesting colours on the cave walls.

FOSSILS

DID YOU KNOW THAT ROCKS CAN TELL US ABOUT THE PAST?

Fossils can form in sedimentary rock. Fossils are the **imprint** of animals and plants that were trapped in sedimentary rock which has hardened over millions of years. A lot of what we know about animals and plants that lived a long time ago has come from fossils.

These **trilobite** fossils were caught in stone over 500 million years ago!

Geologists can use sedimentary rock to tell them lots of different things about the time that it was formed. You could say that the history of the world is written in stone. Maybe you can learn to read it.

GLOSSARY

acidic	contains a chemical substance that causes damage to the natural environment
deposited	to leave something somewhere
dissolved	to have become part of a liquid
groundwater	water held underground in soil or in cracks between rocks
imprint	the indented outline that something leaves when it presses against something else
lava	molten or liquid rock that has surfaced above the Earth's crust
magma	molten or liquid rock below or within the Earth's crust
metallic	containing or appearing like metal
pressure	a continuous physical force exerted on an object, which is caused by something pressing against it
trilobite	an extinct water dwelling creature often found fossilised

INDEX

change 10-11
crystals 7, 9, 11
history 23
mountains 4
pressure 10-11, 13
temperature 10-11
tools 20-21
volcanoes 10
water 9, 13, 15-17, 19